Soul Surgery

Also by Mariel Torres:

The Making Of A Virtuous Woman

Overcoming Fear and Rejection

MARIEL TORRES

Soul Surgery

YOUR HEART MATTERS!

CHALFANT ECKERT
PUBLISHING

ISBN-13: 978-1-63308-108-6 (paperback journal edition)
ISBN-10: 1633081087 (paperback journal edition)
ISBN-13: 978-1-63308-109-3 (ebook)
ISBN-10: 1633081095 (ebook)

Interior Design by R'tor John D. Maghuyop

CHALFANT ECKERT
PUBLISHING

1028 S Bishop Avenue, Dept. 178
Rolla, MO 65401

Printed in United States of America

To My Sisters in Christ

who face trials that seem insurmountable and who long

to experience the healing power of God's love..

TABLE OF CONTENTS

FOREWORD

It is with great pleasure that I pen this foreword for Mariel's new book. I know you will enjoy her insightful revelations on living a full and productive life that honors God and empowers you to be the best you can be.

Mariel speaks with authority based on personal experience. Although she has been a Christian for more than half her three-decade-long life, she like most of us, has struggled with fear, low self-esteem, "man troubles," and other shackles causing her to think she was cursed to a life of unhappiness.

Through scripture, prayer, and listening to the Holy Spirit, Mariel was able to overcome her challenges and step into the abundant life and ministry God planned for her. She is fearfully and wonderfully made and in the center of God's will, making her the perfect coach to lead you to the same place of peace and harmony with yourself, with God, and with your eternal destiny.

This book will confront your erroneous thinking; support your spiritual growth; and ask you to consider your life experiences so that you can revise your attitudes, emotions, and beliefs to align with scripture. Sit back, relax, and join her on a quest to discover your true identity, purpose, and inheritance in Christ. You will be blessed. I know that I was!

—Dr. Kitty Bickford, DBS
Founder, Pasture Valley Children Missions
www.doyourownnonprofit.com

CHAPTER 1

BEAUTY AND THE BEAST

Behold you are beautiful, my love,
behold you are beautiful!

Song of Solomon 4:1, ESV

*B*eauty is in the eye of the beholder, and has been defined as a combination of qualities such as shape, color, and form that please the aesthetic senses, especially the sight, or as denoting something intended to make a woman more attractive (Oxford Online Dictionary, n.d.).

In Disney's *Beauty and the Beast* (Gary Trousdale, 1991), an overindulgent, self-centered, and inconsiderate prince was transformed into an ugly beast as punishment for arrogantly judging people based on appearance, and to teach him to love someone other than himself. He held Belle captive in his dark castle filled with gargoyles and ugly hideous statues. She was considered *Beauty* and only she could free him from the curse he was under, and then only if she could love him in spite of his monstrous appearance.

When I consider this story, I imagine God (living in our true inner self) as *beauty*, while the *beast* is the false outward shell we portray to the world to hide our self-perceived inadequacies and failings. The *beast* represents all the curve balls life has thrown at us, the heartaches we have endured, the silent tears we shed when no one was looking, the molestation and rape of our spirits and self-esteem, the rap and false accusations we have lived through, the feelings of being children without guidance from parents sensitive to our needs, and every other beastly happening that has made us feel worthless and unappreciated.

The *Beast* lived in the West Wing of the castle, but forbid Belle to enter. Shattered photos of happier times and broken mirrors lined the great hall, symbolizing the path our lives sometimes follow leading to broken hearts and dreams. Miserable and angry with his lot in life, he didn't know how to effect the changes needed for him to escape the curse, so felt hopeless and helpless.

There are times when we feel helpless and broken, unable to escape the feelings of hopelessness surrounding the circumstances in our lives. Like the *Beast*, we ask ourselves who could possibly love us in our current condition. The good news is the condition is not permanent. The West Wing was also full of windows, representing illumination and enlightenment, allowing us to see beyond ourselves and the details of our situations, beckoning us to move past the darkness we hide in, and escape from the shame and neglect we experience as we isolate ourselves from the world and from God.

The windows also symbolize opportunities for restoration. Whatever you are battling, whatever holds you captive, whatever seems impossible to overcome, God has already sent a window of restoration, but you must put yourself in the right positon and frame of mind physically, mentally, and spiritually to recognize and accept it. One of the best ways to do that is to let His light shine into the windows of your spirit and soul, which make up the heart. Scripture tells us that His Word is a lamp to our feet and a light to our path (Psalm 119:105). Not everyone accepts that as true, scripture appears foolish to those without God because scripture is spiritually discerned. Without the Holy Spirit's influence, natural man cannot understand the significance of God's Word (1 Corinthians 2:14).

In the *Beauty and the Beast* analogy, the beast permitted his physical state to overshadow his soul and spirit. He had the answer to his problem right there with him, but didn't comprehend it at first because he didn't know how to love Belle or how to make her love him. Isn't that just like life? Sometimes we are right on the threshold of our breakthrough or deliverance, but we cannot obtain it because we let our physical circumstances prevail over our soul and spirit, thus affecting our emotions, judgment, actions, and decision making abilities. The Bible warns us that above all else, we must guard our hearts, for everything we do flows from it (Proverbs 4:23).

BREAKING FREE

So what can you do when you are held captive in a yoke of bondage that feels insurmountable? You can give up and be deceived by the enemy, or you can get yourself in position to be free. For the latter, you must have a little faith!

Faith comes by hearing and hearing by the Word of God (Romans 10:17). You don't need large quantities of faith. Jesus tells us in Matthew 17:20 that, "You don't have enough faith...I tell you the truth, if you had faith even as small as a mustard seed, you could say to this mountain, 'Move from here to there,' and it would move. Nothing would be impossible." Faith is a gift from God, if you don't have it or have enough of it, all you have to do is ask and He will give it to you. A tiny mustard seed can produce a large tree, and a small amount of faith can produce huge results because it holds the power of God. Without faith, it is impossible to please God (Hebrews 11:6).

GETTING INTO POSITION

The *Beast* wasn't restored until he allowed *Beauty* into his dark places, and we are not restored until we allow God to shine His light into our dark places. When we do, we acknowledge to God and ourselves that there is a problem which we are not strong enough to fix without His help, that we are willing to hear from God and receive His intervention, and that we trust God and have faith that He is able and willing to intervene.

When you turn your circumstances over to God, you can expect Him to speak to you through the Holy Spirit and make you aware of the truth behind anything you are doing that is not in alignment with His Word. "For the Word of God is living and active, sharper than any two-edged sword, piercing to the division of soul and of spirit, of joints and of marrow, and discerning the thoughts and intentions of the heart" (Hebrews 4:12). If the soul and spirit make up the heart, then only God can bring a division so that whatever doesn't line up with His Word can be removed so that you will no longer be deceived. You will get to exercise your power to resist the devil so that he will flee from you, and accept the mercy and grace of Jesus Christ to experience a transformed life. By simply repositioning yourself, you can operate according to the rule of God and have power over every area of your life!

M A T T E R S   O F   T H E   H E A R T

1. What yokes of bondage that you are not strong enough to overcome alone are currently holding you captive?

2. What has occurred in your past that still hurts you or causes you fear?

3. What exists in your dark places that affects your emotions, judgment, actions, and decision making abilities?

4. Do you have enough faith or is it time to ask God for more?

5. What would it take for you to trust God to intervene in your life?

Soul Surgery Journal: My Heart's Notes

_____

_____

_____

_____

_____

_____

_____

_____

_____

_____

_____

_____

_____

_____

CHAPTER 2

OPEN THE EYES OF MY HEART

*But let your adorning be the hidden person of the heart with
the imperishable beauty of a gentle and quiet spirit, which in
God's sight is very precious.*

1 Peter 3:4, ESV

*I*t was Sunday morning so let the fashion show begin! I strutted my stuff down the aisle at church in the flyest, most stylish ensemble I could create, right down to the high heels and jewelry. That was how I dealt with the inferiority that was eating me alive inside, I covered up the emptiness and insecurity with external frocks. Always loving fashion, I tried to find the peace I lacked by designing jewelry and putting outfits together that reeked of class and created the attention and approval I deeply longed for.

That Sunday morning everything was falling apart for me. I was confused and angry, sad to the bone, at my lowest, and hated life. I stayed up on Saturday night and designed my first pair of heels and purchased an outfit to match. I just knew I was going to garner the praise of the fashion-conscious souls at church, and the attention was going to lift me out of the mire I was stuck in. But that wasn't what happened.

Before I got to my seat, the woman pastor called me to the front of the church, as if she had been waiting for me to arrive. As I headed

19

that way, a faint thought crossed my mind that this must be how models felt as they swaggered down runways showing off the latest fashions for adoring crowds. I wanted everyone to notice my heels.

YOU CAN RUN BUT YOU CAN'T HIDE

This woman of God came down from the pulpit, looked me in the eye and stated boldly, "There is more to you than what is on the outside. God wants you to surrender what is on the inside, all of it!"

I thought I had surrendered all to God, so her words didn't make much sense to me.

"Run Mariel, run to the back of the church and by the time you get there, God is going to break away all those things that are hindering you."

Her words bewildered me. I thought I was cute and attractive and didn't want to run, so I just kind of speed walked to the back of the church, trying to maintain my dignity and retain the vogue of my attire.

She shouted, "Get back down here and do it again. This time run like you are running for your life!"

Obediently I returned and this time, I ran as hard as I could. The power of the Holy Spirit came upon me and I raised my arms toward heaven and cried out to God.

She told me to run one more time saying, "You are running for God. From this day forward, nothing or no one is going to be able to stop you."

Before I could get back to her, the glory of God through the Holy Spirit fell upon me and I went down, my materialistic flesh and bones unable to stand in God's presence.

Nothing around me was clear or important but on some level I heard the pastor say, "Every generational curse is broken, and every hidden hurt is exposed and must flee in the name of Jesus."

While I laid there unaware of my surroundings, God brought to mind her word of knowledge from two years earlier, similar to the one she had just given me. Later when I got up off the floor, I was a mess.

My hair was disheveled, my skirt twisted, the jewels and feathers from my shoes were everywhere, and my makeup smeared all over my face from the Holy Spirit's outpouring of tears. I didn't care and neither did God! He wasn't one bit concerned with my outward appearance, but instead my inner condition. I felt light and free and released from the burden of the negative emotional baggage I had carried, I left it there in the aisle. It was as if God put me in a new skin, and I felt a sense of peace that I had been longing for. I knew God was concerned about me, enough to stop a service and provide my window of opportunity for freedom.

About two weeks later, a further revelation from the Lord helped me to understand that I had been blinded to real beauty (God's love) so had been walking around in defeat. The Holy Spirit revealed to me that the devil was a thief and a liar, and the thief came only to steal and kill and destroy, but Jesus came that I may have life and have it abundantly (John 10:10).

So I was cleansed from the influence of unclean spirits, and felt that I was once again all right, in control, and able to face challenges alone. What folly! When God cleanses you, you must make an effort to stay clean. You have to stay in His Word, surround yourself with other believers, and bathe your life in prayer so that you remain so full of God that there is no room for the enemy to plague you. I am reminded of the story of an unclean spirit that was banished from a man. The scripture says that the unclean spirit will "return to my house from which it came; and when it comes, it finds it unoccupied, swept, and put in order. Then it goes and takes along with it seven other spirits more wicked than itself, and they go in and live there; and the last state of that man becomes worse than the first" (Matthew 12:44-45). This scripture refers to an unsaved person, and although Christians cannot be indwelled with demons, they can be influenced by unclean spirits if they make place for them. God puts a hedge of protection around believers and admonishes them to put on His armor so that they can stand firm and avoid the temptations that lead to bondage.

I messed up and went back into hibernation, rejecting frequent fellowship with the children of God. Again confused, I felt picked on and attacked by everyone, and that nobody cared about or loved me. This may have been a test of my surrender because Satan is the father of confusion, and God is the author and finisher of our faith. But I trusted God although I was going through a difficult time in my Christian walk, mostly caused by my attitude and thoughts.

I began to pray Psalm 51:10, "Create in me a clean heart, O God, and renew a right spirit within me." I wanted God to mold and shape me, make me over, release me from the pressure I felt on every side from the enemy, and restore the freedom so short lived from the recent encounter with the Holy Spirit in church that Sunday morning.

I became clay on a potter's wheel, and of course, God was the potter. He did as I asked and began to mold me and make me into His image. God controlled every facet of the transformation He worked in me. At first I was just a lump of clay that by His hands He shaped, added just the right amount of moisture to, and controlled the speed of the potter's wheel. By letting God remain in control of my life, the vessel He created didn't dry out, crack, or spin out of control, instead becoming a great work of art in progress. This time I didn't rush Him to complete His work in me knowing that if He did, I would end up back on the potter's wheel in the future when the next attack of the enemy came. Willingness to stay on the wheel was my way of showing God I had surrendered to Him and His will for my life. I gave Him permission to make me more like Him, agreeing to die to self, and to become more alive in Christ. I acknowledged that I had no power to change myself, that I needed His power to deliver me. My key to staying on that wheel was constant prayer, not just when things were going wrong, but when all was well too. I took to heart the scripture that says to pray without ceasing (1 Thessalonians 5:17).

THROUGH THE FIRE

Clay must be fired in an oven or kiln to be useful and to reveal flaws, cracks and imperfections. I started through the fire when I was invited to a revival one night. I really didn't feel like going, but something inside pushed me to attend. Figured I would sit in the back so I could leave early if the notion struck me, but the usher sat me on the front row. The guest speaker called me to the front, then told me to step back. I did. Three times!

I thought he was trying to embarrass me in front of all those people, but he said, "God has much work for you. He is cleansing you from the inside out." I didn't understand.

Later at home, I talked with God until I fell sound asleep. He gave me a vision, a room full of hearts representing many aspects of my life, specifically from my childhood. The evangelist told me to step back repeatedly, but he wasn't referring to stepping back physically, he wanted me to step back emotionally and spiritually. Now God was taking me back in this nocturnal vision, revealing to me the hidden hurts and unforgiveness in my heart left over from childhood.

God disclosed to me that I had been reacting to hurt and rejection I had never dealt with. Instead, I tried to hide it under makeup, clothes, and hairstyles which only masked my difficulty in understanding why the hurts occurred. I had let the wrong things go unattended in my heart. Bitterness was deeply rooted and God had to help me work through it so that I could get on with life and leave the emotional baggage back there in that childhood room full of hearts.

GUARD YOUR HEART

I was so busy blaming others for my hurt and pain that I failed to guard my heart. Opening up all those old wounds from many sources over many years caused pain and an abundance of tears. I cried easily anyway, but when I opened Pandora's Box of lifetime hurts, I soaked my pillow often working through it all. The bitterness and hurt that came to the surface left me vulnerable to instant anger, feelings of rejection, and expectation of being mistreated again.

Over time, I came to understand that life is not your circumstances, background, wardrobe, appearance, or bank account. None of those things give you peace. That was not an overnight revelation, it was a process. I had been walking proof that you can dress yourself up and still be miserable. Thanks to the Holy Spirit, I learned to guard my heart and deal with emotional hurts when they came up instead of covering them up.

GOD'S TUG

I have given birth to four children by cesarean section. This major abdominal surgery begins with an incision at the bottom of the stomach that gets progressively deeper with repeated cuts through the layers of skin, exercising care not to nick or cut a blood vessel. One of these procedures was taking an exorbitant amount of time compared to previous births. I got worried, began to cry, and eventually got angry because I didn't know what was taking so long and why they were pulling and tugging on me and the baby. I knew something must be very wrong. As it turned out, those in attendance were mostly medical students practicing on me and my baby. It took forty five minutes to get my son out! Had I been given the choice to have medical students performing the operation, I would have declined.

I said all that to say this:

1. Find out who you are letting perform surgery on you! You want Godly counsel involved in your spiritual operations.

2. Patience is vital when God is performing surgery on us. He will tug and pull on our insides until he removes all uncleanness and trouble spots to restore us to spiritual health.

3. Stop complaining, crying, and getting mad. When God has a scalpel in hand, we need to let Him finish the good work He has begun in us. If we try to circumvent His efforts, it would be like us getting off the operating table before being sewn up. Healing and deliverance would be impossible. The children of Israel took 40 years instead of days to reach the Promised

Land, a whole generation had to die, because of their unbelief and disobedience to God. We must allow the Great Physician to perform heart surgery on us so that we can walk in the joy and peace He has for us instead of wandering aimlessly.

LISTENING TO YOUR HEART

Developing self-control and getting my thoughts under submission was harder than I anticipated. I wanted to let go of the hurts, forgive the trespassers, and move on with my life. However, much like an addict in rehab, I started paying attention to my feelings instead of burying them and was frequently filled with anxiety that I didn't know how to process. I found it helped to capture my thoughts first thing in the morning through prayer and meditation. I had to learn to empty out my emotions, holding nothing back, releasing my fear and nervousness by turning them over to God and asking Him to release me from the worry of the process.

A PRAYER OF RELEASE

My Dearest Heavenly Father,

Thank you for allowing me to come boldly to the Throne of Grace and make my petitions known to you. I enter into your gates with thanksgiving and your courts with praise. Blessed be the name of the Lord who is the same yesterday, today, and forever.

Father, your Word says that you have not given me a spirit of fear which can lead to infirmity, but of power and of love and of a sound mind. I no longer want to be a prisoner in my own skin, I want to be free in you Lord and I want to be filled with more of you. I bind the spirit of denial and release the spirit of truth. I open myself up to you God and ask that you restore the years lost to the locusts, and restore my repentant heart to the place of blessing. You are no respecter of persons and love to give good gifts to your children.

Your Word assures me that no weapon formed against me will prosper; that I can live without fear because you will uphold me with your righteous right hand; that you are my refuge and strength, a very present help in time of trouble; and that all things work together for good for those who love you and are called according to your purpose.

Father I have struggled while denying and hiding the hurts accumulated throughout my lifetime. I ask you to release me from the emotional hold those events have had on me and allow me to let go and receive your healing and your peace that passes all understanding. You are the Great Physician and nothing is too hard for God. Teach me to forgive as you have forgiven me.

You are my rock and my fortress and I put all my trust in you. Thank you for healing and freedom.

In the mighty name of Jesus,
Amen.

MATTERS OF THE HEART

1. What hurts from the past are you carrying around that may be influencing your walk with God and your relationship with others?

2. Who has hurt you that you have not yet forgiven?

3. What keeps you from letting go of the hurt? Fear? Self-righteous indignation? Pride? Stubbornness? Not sure how to let go?

4. How can God help you release the negative emotions associated with the past events that hurt you? What do you want Him to do?

5. What are the best and worst outcomes you would expect if you chose to resolve the issues that hold you captive?

    a. Best
    b. Worst
    c. Other possible outcomes

6. Failing to forgive affects your physical body, your mental state of mind, and the hardness of your heart much more than it affects the person you won't forgive. It also affects your walk with God because He forgives your trespasses as you forgive those who trespass against you. How would the worse outcome be any worse than carrying the unforgiveness and hurt?

7. What would change if you forgave those who hurt you?

8. What are you waiting for?

Soul Surgery Journal: My Heart's Notes

_____

_____

_____

_____

_____

_____

_____

_____

_____

_____

_____

_____

_____

CHAPTER 3

LIVING COUNTERFEIT LIVES

If we confess our sins, He is faithful and just
to forgive us our sins and to cleanse us
from all unrighteousness.

1 John 1:9

*D*id you ever want something so badly that you spent weeks, months, or years pursuing a goal or person in hopes that when you succeeded, you would be happy or complete? You are not alone. Many people try to find happiness by reaching out through their emptiness for things and people they hope will fill them with pleasure. If the pursuit is not God's will, all that effort will produce only momentary fleeting pleasure. If instead you delight yourself in the Lord, He will give you the desires of your heart (Psalm 37:4).

I recall a time when I wanted to fit into a group of Christian women. I made conscious, continuous efforts to blend in, and began to sound and talk like them. I really wanted to belong to their group, but it didn't work. You can't make yourself fit in where you don't belong, no matter how much you struggle and strive. My family, friends, even my pastor noticed that I wasn't acting like myself anymore.

Finally my sister asked me, "Who are you? It's like I don't know you anymore."

She was right. I took on the beliefs, attitudes, and philosophies of the group I tried to assimilate into, and in the process became a fake, not living the authentic life God gave me, but instead exhibiting a counterfeit personality that was not me. Counterfeit is imitation with the intent to deceive (Oxford Online Dictionary, n.d.). Scripture tells me that I am fearfully and wonderfully made (Psalm 139:14), but I thought I could improve on God's design by trying to be more like the women in that group. I should have known that I was automatically second best when I tried to be someone else or someone I was not.

EFFECTS OF SIN

We fail to live authentic, God-inspired and God-directed lives when we venture off into sin and live counterfeit or fake existences. It is easy to do, often starting out innocent and harmless with no intent to grieve the Holy Spirit. But as Pastor Charles Stanley so eloquently stated, "Sin takes you farther than you want to go and keeps you longer than you want to stay." It has commonly been added that it also costs more than you want to pay. For instance, think back to Genesis with Adam and Eve in the Garden of Eden. The serpent beguiled Eve to eat the fruit of the Tree of Knowledge of Good and Evil. She didn't have to, she knew better, but when the serpent put his counterfeit spin on what God commanded, both she and Adam ate the fruit and their eyes were immediately opened. The consequences included every human since being born with a sin nature, and ultimately Jesus coming to die on the cross in our stead as a propitiation (sacrifice of atonement) for our sins. Adam and Eve knew better! They walked with God in the cool of the evening, lived in a perfect environment, and wanted for nothing. What happened?

Although not logical, Adam and Eve were presented with a choice and they made the wrong decision. Often we do the same thing, entering or persisting in sin knowing it is wrong and doesn't match up to God's will. The scripture says "a little leaven leavens the whole lump" (Galatians 5:9), meaning that once you enter into sin, the consequences are broad, the effects spread to other areas, and it is easy to go deeper before you realize it. God gives us free will because He wants us to serve Him voluntarily. Even when we know better, we sometimes make the wrong choice because we are looking for transient counterfeit rewards we think will make us happy. We think we can get away with sin and escape detection and consequences. Even when we try to hide our sin and present a fake façade to the world, eventually we will be found out. The Bible says, "For nothing is hidden that will not be made manifest, nor is anything secret that will not be known and come to light" (Luke 8:17). Our particular circumstances are not unique or exempt from detection and outcome. God did not create us to live in deception, but in His likeness and image. Even when we try to sugarcoat them with excuses and rationalizations, our sins will find us out (Numbers 32:23).

REPENT!

Sin breaks our fellowship with and separates us from God. The more we sin, the further away we get from God. He doesn't leave us, He stays right where we left Him and waits for us to return. It is up to us to turn around and come back to Him. To help us make the right decision, the Holy Spirit's still small voice speaks to our spirits, convicting us of sin and wooing us back into the fold and fellowship with God.

God is not opposed to pleasure, but He wants us to have an abundant Christian life that is free of sin. We can have a life of happiness and pleasure with God's DNA in our veins and a peace that passes all understanding. When we are in Christ, we are new creatures. Old things pass away, and all things are new (2 Corinthians 5:17). We don't need to sin anymore to have fun.

When we have been in our sins and trespasses but turn around and choose the straight and narrow Christian walk and place our sins under the blood of Jesus Christ, we *repent*, or turn away from our sins. The Bible admonishes us to "repent therefore, and turn back, that your sins may be blotted out" (Acts 3:19). Sin feels pleasant for a season (Hebrews 11:25), and the wages of sin is death, but the free gift of God is eternal life in Christ Jesus our Lord (Romans 6:23). The gate is wide and the way is easy that leads to destruction, and those who enter by it are many. For the gate is narrow and the way is hard that leads to life, and those who find it are few (Matthew 7:13-14).

Scripture says to resist the devil and he will flee from you (James 4:7). Easily said, harder to actually do. We must train ourselves to resist at the first thought or inclination to sin. Temptation is normal and to be expected, but as God's children, we are more than conquerors (Romans 8:37), and we can do all things through Christ who strengthens us (Philippians 4:13). If we stay in God's Word, allow the Holy Spirit to guide us, pray often seeking God's face and His will, and guard our hearts against all unrighteousness, we will be clean and He will abide in us (John 15:3-4), but it is our free will choice.

YOUR HEART MATTERS

1. Think back over your life. What things or people have you pursued that once acquired did not give you the long term happiness you expected?

2. What or who are you pursuing now that is out of God's will? Why are you pursuing it or them? Why is it out of God's will?

3. Recall a time you changed to fit in, even if you didn't really belong. How did you feel after the initial euphoria? How did it end? Was it worth it? Why or why not? What did you learn?

4. How prone are you to willful sin? Is it in just one or two areas that you are particularly weak in or is it universal? What can you do to resist the temptation? How would your life change if you were to get the victory over this or these willful sins?

5. Pastor Charles Stanley stated, "Sin takes you farther than you want to go and keeps you longer than you want to stay." Do you agree or disagree? What personal experience influences your answer?

Soul Surgery Journal: My Heart's Notes

_____

_____

_____

_____

_____

_____

_____

_____

_____

_____

_____

_____

_____

_____

CHAPTER 4

UNFORGIVENESS

Father, forgive them,
for they know not what they do.

Luke 23:24, ESV

ver try to forgive someone but couldn't seem to let go of the hurt and resentment? Or you were secretly unwilling to forgive because you didn't think the person deserved it? Or you refused to forgive because you didn't receive an apology and were not asked to forgive? Forgiveness is one of the most difficult undertakings of Christianity to master, and even to their detriment, some people never develop the ability to forgive.

Unforgiveness has widespread consequences, and that is one of the big reasons the enemy keeps resentment alive in your thoughts and emotions. In Deborah Finley's book, *What Your Future Holds and What You Can Do to Change It,* she explains:

Unforgiveness distresses your muscular-skeletal system by increasing forehead muscle tension, thereby producing headaches, and by also producing other symptoms: stomach aches, muscle tension, joint pain/aches, dizziness and tiredness. For example, your muscles may tighten, causing imbalances or pain in your neck, back and limbs. There is decreased blood flow to the joint surfaces. This makes it more difficult for the blood to remove wastes from the tissues. It reduces the supply of oxygen and nutrients to the cells. This increases chances of delayed or inadequate repair during sleep, impairing recovery from injury, arthritis, etc. It can cause your teeth to clench at night contributing to problems with your teeth and jaw joints. Injury through inattention, accident, or violence is more likely. The peptide and hormonal chemical "messengers" are altered in every system of the body. The blood flow to your heart is constricted. Your digestion is impaired (Xulon Press, 2007).

Is it any wonder that God wants and expects us to forgive others? Holding onto grudges, resentment, and bitterness negatively affects you, even when it doesn't bother the person you must forgive. Like a deadly contagious disease, unforgiveness causes a root of bitterness to spring up infecting the people around you too (Hebrews 12:15).

The Lord's Prayer asks God to forgive us our debts (or trespasses) as we forgive those who trespass against us (Matthew 6:12). Whether you say *debts* or *trespasses*, both mean *sin*, and that is what we must forgive. It is a conscious choice to release the anger and hurt and give up the hold it has on you. Only then can you experience God's peace and joy in your life. If you have trouble forgiving, remember that God forgave you all your trespasses and threw them into the sea of forgetfulness (Micah 7:19), removed your transgressions as far as the east is from the west (Psalm 103:12), and cast your sins behind His back (Isaiah 38:17). Not just one sin one time, but all sins for all time: all the wretched public and private sins of a lifetime. If He is willing to do that unconditionally for you, what excuse do you have not to forgive someone of their one or two or ten transgressions?

Peter asked Jesus, "Lord, how often will my brother sin against me, and I forgive him? As many as seven times?" (Matthew 18:21).

Jesus said to him, "I do not say to you seven times, but seventy-seven times." (Matthew 8:22).

In other words, it is your duty to continue to forgive even with multiple hurts and offenses against you. If you fail to forgive others their trespasses, neither will God forgive yours (Matthew 6:15). Forgiveness is a matter not of convenience or preference, but of obedience. Forgiving does not mean you have to like who you forgave, or fellowship with them, or trust them ever again. It simply means you are not willing to let their behavior infect your heart any longer. The Bible tells you that "If your brother sins against you, go and tell him his fault, between you and him alone. If he listens to you, you have gained your brother" (Matthew 18:15). If you cannot turn the page in the relationship, you can close the book and move on. And although you cannot control what others do, you can control what you do, say, and think. Choosing to take control and forgive is a gift you give to yourself, which restores you to fellowship with God.

YOUR HEART MATTERS

1. What hurt(s) are you hanging onto that you need to let go?

2. What keeps you from forgiving?

3. What are you getting out of holding on to the hurt or anger?

4. What would be the worst thing to happen if you chose to forgive?

5. What is the best thing that could happen if you forgave?

6. How would your life, health, attitude, and relationships improve if you chose to forgive?

7. What happens if you do not forgive? How will you justify that conscious decision before God one day?

Soul Surgery Journal: My Heart's Notes

CHAPTER 5

PULLING DOWN STRONGHOLDS

Bless those who persecute you; bless and do not curse.

Romans 12:14, ESV

*H*ave you ever felt like you were under a curse of some kind because you continued to struggle with the same kinds of issues repeatedly and nothing was resolved? We all feel that way occasionally, but once you understand the nature of Bible curses, you will be relieved.

The Old Testament talks of many curses starting back as far as Genesis. God cursed the serpent causing him to crawl on his belly, the ground causing man to till the soil by the sweat of his brow, and women causing them to bring forth children in pain. He put a curse on Cain for killing Abel, and Noah cursed Ham for looking on his father's nakedness with disrespect.

God told Abraham, "I will bless those who bless you, and him who dishonors you I will curse, and in you all the families of the earth shall be blessed" (Genesis 12:3). God vowed to deal with the nations of the earth based on how they treated Abraham and his offspring (Israel). Isaac gave the same blessing to his son Jacob. Job cursed the day he was born. Goliath cursed David by the names of his heathen gods. We know the outcome of that arrogance. Joshua cursed the Gibeonites to slavery because of their treachery against Israel. All those curses were applied to particular circumstances and people based on their actions, and were predictions and prophecy, not sorcery and witchcraft.

Proverbs tells us that if we give to the poor we will be blessed, and if we don't, we are cursed. Malachi spells out that if we do not tithe, we are robbing God, so are cursed with a curse. The Ten Commandments and other scriptures extol the virtue of honoring our fathers and mothers, with a curse of a shorter life (and the death penalty in Leviticus 20:9) if we dishonor them.

There were several curses specifically for the Jewish people:

All these curses shall come upon you and pursue you and overtake you till you are destroyed, because you did not obey the voice of the LORD your God, to keep His commandments and His statutes that he commanded you. They shall be a sign and a wonder against you and your offspring forever. (Deuteronomy 28:45-46).

You shall not bow down to them or serve them, for I the LORD your God am a jealous God, visiting the iniquity of the fathers on the children to the third and the fourth generation of those who hate me (Exodus 20:5).

The LORD passed before him and proclaimed, "The LORD, the LORD, a God merciful and gracious, slow to anger, and abounding in steadfast love and faithfulness, keeping steadfast love for thousands, forgiving iniquity and transgression and sin, but who will by no means clear the guilty, visiting the iniquity of the fathers on the children and the children's children, to the third and the fourth generation" (Exodus 34:6-7).

The LORD is slow to anger and abounding in steadfast love, forgiving iniquity and transgression, but he will by no means clear the guilty, visiting the iniquity of the fathers on the children, to the third and the fourth generation (Numbers 14:18).

Each of the curses for Israel was based on idol worship without repentance. If a man bowed down to strange gods and did not return to the Lord after being given the chance to repent, then the iniquities of the father were visited on the children, grandchildren, great grandchildren, and great-great grandchildren. The penalty for idolatry was severe with long term effects.

The good news is we are not subject to those generational curses. Ezekiel 18:20 tells us, "The soul who sins shall die. The son shall not suffer for the iniquity of the father, nor the father suffer for the iniquity of the son. The righteousness of the righteous shall be upon himself, and the wickedness of the wicked shall be upon himself."

So why is it that negative things seem to happen generation after generation in your family? Not because of a curse, but because today's decisions determine our tomorrows, and yesterday's decisions determined today. Galatians 6:7 counsels, "Do not be deceived: God is not mocked, for whatever one sows, that will he also reap." If you plant and water tomato seeds, you can expect tomatoes to come up. Likewise, if you take drugs, you can expect to become addicted. If you overeat, you are going to get fat.

So how does that play out over generations? If you came from a long line of alcoholics, chances are you have been exposed to alcohol and are vulnerable to that addiction. If your family has been steeped in poverty for generations, it could be that lack of education has limited job opportunities and everyone is stuck in low income occupations due to lack of training. If criminal behavior was prevalent in your lineage, most likely attitudes toward authority and moral issues were passed down causing history to repeat itself. If many people in your lineage contracted cancer, high blood pressure, diabetes, or other life changing diseases, perhaps it was because they all shared similar lifestyles such as lack of exercise, poor diet, anger management issues, unwise risk taking, and other influences that have nothing to do with being under a curse.

If you understand that Bible curses were under the law, then Galatians 3:13 relieves your concern about being under a curse, "Christ redeemed us from the curse of the law by becoming a curse for us…" He died on the cross for our sins, taking our place, paying our sin debt that so we are no longer under the curse of the law. Instead, we are under grace – the unmerited favor of the holy God through Christ Jesus. "For by grace you have been saved through faith. And this is not your own doing; it is the gift of God, not a result of works, so that no one may boast" (Ephesians 2:8-9).

What can you do to demonstrate your appreciation to God and to Jesus for this free gift? Here are just a few things scripture says go along with the Christian life (not as works, they do not get you into heaven, but as part of your Christian walk because you are grateful for God's unmerited favor):

- Repent of your sins.

- Put on the whole armor of God so that you can fight with spiritual weapons: gird your loins with truth; put on the breastplate of righteousness; shod your feet with the preparation of the gospel of peace; take the shield of faith, the helmet of salvation, and the Sword of the Spirit which is the Word of God.

- Forgive those who hurt you and despitefully use you.

- Develop and maintain a Godly attitude by renewing with the Word of God daily.

- Let your words be evidence of your faith.

- Walk in obedience.

- You will make mistakes for we all fall short of the glory of God, but surrender your heart to God and learn from your mistakes.

- Worship, praise, and pray so that you will be empowered and strengthened by the Holy Spirit.

- Let your light shine in a dark world of sin. Let the Fruit of the Spirit (yes, it is singular, not plural) show in all you do by displaying love, joy, peace, patience, kindness, goodness, faithfulness, gentleness, and self-control.

• Remember that no matter what happens, God will never leave you or forsake you, even if your father, husband, wife, mother, or best friend do. He won't. He is faithful even when others (including you) are not.

Your Heart Matters

1. What were you taught about generational curses?

2. Have you ever felt you were under a curse? What were the circumstances that caused you to think so?

3. What other explanation exists to explain what looked like a curse?

4. What seeds are you sowing now that could cause you to reap negatively in the future?

5. How can you change the outcome?

Soul Surgery Journal: My Heart's Notes

CHAPTER 6

NOT OF THE WORLD

He came to His own,
and His own people did not receive Him.

John 1:11, ESV

*I*t is no surprise that when you begin to change, people around you notice. Some commend you, others ridicule your efforts to walk the walk on your God-directed Christian journey. They might say things like, "Who does she think she is?" or "He thinks he is better than us!" What people say about you won't be nearly as bad as what they said about Jesus. Mark 6:4 weighs in with "A prophet is not without honor, except in his hometown and among his relatives and in his own household." People in Nazareth thought Jesus was a carpenter and scoffed, criticized, and mocked His divine heritage and mission. Because of their unbelief, he did few miracles near His home, instead going other places where people were willing to hear the gospel and surrender to its message. You can expect no less. Unbelievers sneer at you and accuse you of "getting religion," as if giving your heart to the Lord was some condition of trickery that only simple minded people fall prey to.

Human reasoning is limited because…it is human! Therefore take counsel from the Word of God because the author and finisher of our faith knows the beginning from the end, unlike those who chide you with disapproval for your beliefs. You are not in this world to please them, you are here to please God and do His will. "All that will live godly in Christ Jesus shall suffer persecution" (2 Timothy 3:12).

So how exactly do you turn a deaf ear when someone makes fun of you and your beliefs? Max Lucado wrote in *Facing Your Giants*, "You select the voices you hear. Why give ear to pea-brains and scoffers when you can, with the same ear, listen to the voice of God?" (2006, p. 105). John 10:27 reminds us that "My sheep hear my voice, and I know them, and they follow me."

Perhaps the best way to handle the naysayers is as Philip handled it when Nathanael said, "Can anything good come out of Nazareth?" (John 1:46). Philip simply replied, "Come and see." He didn't try to convince Nathanael, he asked him to research the matter, and come to His own conclusions based on observation and fact. Many people's minds are biased against any religious belief, and the only way they will get over the prejudice (which is pre-judgment) is to have a personal encounter with the Savior. All your words won't mean a thing. Until that encounter, they may consider you a hypocrite, or think that you being a new creature in Christ is an act that will end when you get tired of putting on a temporary show. You know it is not a show, and you must continue in the faith. Matthew 5:16 instructs, "Let your light shine before others, so that they may see your good works and give glory to your Father who is in heaven."

There is much counsel in scripture about how to conduct yourself around people who don't know Christ. They may be antagonistic or just skeptical, but either way, it may be your consistent, unwavering example that eventually silences their objections and leads them to salvation. Titus 2:7-8 tells us, "Show yourself in all respects to be a model of good works and in your teaching show integrity, dignity, and sound speech that cannot be condemned, so that an opponent may be put to shame, having nothing evil to say about us."

Remember who you are in Christ. "You are a chosen race, a royal priesthood, a holy nation, a people for His own possession, that you may proclaim the excellencies of him who called you out of darkness into His marvelous light" (1 Peter 2:9). Need I say more?

YOUR HEART MATTERS

1. Recall instances when people poked fun or scoffed at your faith.

   a. What issue did they raise?
   b. Why (if you know) did they raise it?
   c. How did you feel?
   d. What did you do about it?
   e. How did it change your relationship with them?
   f. What was the eventual outcome?

2. Think about the next time someone calls your Christian walk into question. List some ways you can handle it that would be pleasing to God.

3. How can you witness to people without alienating them about how God called you out of darkness into His wonderful light?

Soul Surgery Journal: My Heart's Notes

_____

_____

_____

_____

_____

_____

_____

_____

_____

_____

_____

_____

_____

CHAPTER 7

HEARING HIS VOICE

Be still and know that I am God.

Psalm 46:10, ESV

*I*t is easy to get weighed down and overwhelmed with daily routines and responsibilities. Even heavier to carry are the feelings of inferiority we harbor when those we thought cared hurt or abandon us. We feel powerless, afraid, rejected, shameful, unworthy, and/or guilty. At those times, it is common to place value on what we think and how circumstances make us feel, but it is hard to think straight or experience positive feelings when we are overloaded with cares or heartbreak. Emotions are deceptive, fueled by fears and hopes causing us to make desperate choices. Jeremiah 17:9 says it like this, "The heart is deceitful above all things, and desperately sick; who can understand it?" Isn't that true? If not, we wouldn't keep taking back that no-good abusive man who lies and cheats on us. Because we lack objectivity in times of emotional stress, we cannot lean on our own understanding, it may be faulty under pressure. Instead, we must look to our Heavenly Father to lead, guide, and direct us.

The good news is that heaven never closes! God doesn't take days off or pick and choose when to be there for us, and never gets tired of dealing with us and our problems, even when we are considered a pain by others. He is faithful to never leave or forsake us, and we can always depend on Him to be a voice of reason in the midst of confusion. God is our refuge and strength, a very present help in trouble (Psalm 46:1).

Sadly, some people are scared to talk with God, or only talk to Him when they are in trouble, and still others pray long lists of wants and desires as if He were Santa Claus or Daddy Warbucks instead of the Lord of heaven and earth. We often relate to Him based on our relationship with our earthly fathers, who are human and far from perfect. We are not lost without our parents or pastor, but we are lost without our Heavenly Father and High Priest. I wonder how God feels when His children are afraid of him, ignore Him unless they are in a predicament, or want what is in His hand instead of what is in His heart. As a parent, I would be grieved if my children treated me in those ways and communication was limited by those factors.

The primary method of communication with God is prayer and the Bible has much to say about it, even spelling out some prayers for our edification. One of the key insights gleaned from reading the Bible is that we get God's attention when we "Enter His gates with thanksgiving, and His courts with praise! Give thanks to him; bless His name!" (Psalm 100:4). It doesn't get much easier than that. Philippians 4:6 tells us, "Do not be anxious about anything, but in everything by prayer and supplication with thanksgiving let your requests be made known to God." The theme is obvious: Pray with a thankful heart and God will listen.

The book of James has much to say that helps us understand the necessity and blessing of communicating with God through prayer:

- Is anyone among you suffering? Let him pray (James 5:13).

- Is anyone cheerful? Let him sing praise (James 5:13).

- Is anyone among you sick? Let him call for the elders of the church, and let them pray over him, anointing him with oil in the name of the Lord. And the prayer of faith will save the one who is sick, and the Lord will raise him up. And if he has committed sins, he will be forgiven. Therefore, confess your sins to one another and pray for one another, that you may be healed (James 5:14-16).

- The prayer of a righteous person has great power as it is working (James 5:16).

Unlike the children of Israel who had to go to the priest and bring sin, peace, burnt or trespass offerings, Christians have God's permission to come boldly to the Throne of Grace that they may obtain mercy and find grace to help in time of need (Hebrews 4:16). Instead of spotless lambs, rams, and doves, ours is a sacrifice of praise.

Many people think they are too busy to pray. If you realize that you don't have to bow your head and close your eyes to pray or spend long periods of time in prayer, many more opportunities to commune and communicate with God appear. If you have a minute that you could pick up your phone and call your earthly father, you have time to call your Heavenly Father. If you have time to text or tweet your friend or brother, you have time to talk with the friend who sticks closer than a brother (Proverbs 18:24). You can pray while driving, eating lunch, shopping, filling up your car with gas, or waiting in line to check out at Walmart. Have you ever set aside a specific time to visit with a family member? Maybe Saturday morning with your grandmother or Sunday night with your sister? You can also set aside time to visit with God. He will enjoy that one-on-one time with you and consider it just as special as your earthly dad does.

God also communicates with us through His Word. The Bible is alive and full of answers to life's dilemmas. Oprah, Facebook friends, and Dr. Phil don't always have the answers, but God's Word does. No matter how often you read it, there is always be something new that you didn't see or understand before, as if the needed scriptures come to life for you at just the right time. All Scripture is breathed out by God and profitable for teaching, for reproof, for correction, and for training in righteousness that the man of God may be complete, equipped for every good work (2 Timothy 3:16-17).

Some scriptures are hard to swallow and harder to digest, but are there for mature Christians to chew on and learn from. Hebrews 5:14 educates us, "But solid food is for the mature, for those who have their powers of discernment trained by constant practice to distinguish good from evil."

God communicates with us at times through other believers. Chance conversations are no accident, God directs our path. He gives us Christian friends to consult with. "Where there is no guidance, a people falls, but in an abundance of counselors there is safety" (Proverbs 11:14). Likewise, we must be careful when receiving a word of knowledge, wisdom, or prophecy to make sure it is of the Lord. God will give us discernment through His Word and the Holy Spirit so that we can rightly divide the Word of truth and know if it is of God.

God also communicates with us through the Holy Spirit, who dwells within us and comforts us. He speaks to us with a still, small voice. In other words, he whispers to our hearts. Many times I have asked him to speak louder instead of hitting me with a brick to get my attention. The Holy Spirit never points to himself, only to Jesus. "Likewise the Spirit helps us in our weakness. For we do not know what to pray for as we ought, but the Spirit himself intercedes for us with groanings too deep for words" (Romans 8:26).

With so many avenues available to have true dialog with our Heavenly Father, isn't it time to shut off the television, shut down the computer, put the iPad away, turn off the smart phone, the get alone in your prayer closet, humble your heart, and get in true relationship with your eternal father? His Word is plain, "Ask, and it will be given to you; seek, and you will find; knock, and it will be opened to you" (Matthew 7:7). What are you waiting for?

YOUR HEART MATTERS

1. Think about your personal experience with Jeremiah 17:9, "The heart is deceitful above all things, and desperately sick; who can understand it?" Do you agree or disagree? Why?

2. Recall a time when you leaned on your own understanding instead of God's Word. What happened? What did you learn?

3. How has your relationship with your earthly father influenced your relationship with your Heavenly Father?

4. Think about your communication with God. Assign percentages to each of the following methods so that the total equals 100%. What do your answers reveal about your relationship with God?

    a. Prayer
    b. Reading scripture
    c. Interacting with Christian brothers and sisters
    d. Listening to the Holy Spirit

5. Think about your schedule. When can you include God in your life during other pursuits?

Soul Surgery Journal: My Heart's Notes

_____

_____

_____

_____

_____

_____

_____

_____

_____

_____

_____

_____

_____

_____

_____

CHAPTER 8

A NEW HEART

And I will give you a new heart, and a new spirit I will put within you. And I will remove the heart of stone from your flesh and give you a heart of flesh.

Ezekiel 36:26, ESV

nbelievers and some believers have serious heart disease and suffer from a bad spiritual heart condition that if left untreated will end in spiritual death and eternity in hell. It is an unnecessary fatality when God is not willing that any should perish and that all come to the saving knowledge of Christ (2 Peter 3:8). No one has to die of a spiritual heart attack or stroke, especially when we have the Great Physician who will not only perform a spiritual heart transplant, but will also donate His own heart to us.

When you allow God to give you a heart transplant, some things will change and some will stay the same. In Juanita Bynum's *Matters of the Heart* (2002) she writes, "According to medicine, the heart transplant is immediate, but the mind transformation is progressive" (p. 151). True in a physical heart transplant, but also true in a spiritual transplant. You can still expect temptation, but also expect that "No temptation has overtaken you that is not common to man. God is faithful, and he will not let you be tempted beyond your ability, but with the temptation he will also provide the way of escape, that you may be able to endure it" (1 Corinthians 10:13).

You can expect to encounter all the same urges, drives, instincts, and compulsions you had before, and God knows you will make mistakes as you mature in Christ. Just as a loving father would, God still cares about you when you fail, and He will pick you up, dust you off, and console you. "For the LORD sees not as man sees: man looks on the outward appearance, but the LORD looks on the heart" (1 Samuel 16:7).

Circumstances and life happenings won't change; there will still be heartache, grief, stress, loss, and difficulty to contend with. At first you may be tempted to respond the same way you did with your old heart, but the Holy Spirit will convict you of poor handling with His still small voice speaking to you through God's heart. Over time, the way you respond verbally, mentally, and emotionally will change because your sin nature has been forgiven and replaced with pure motives. You might be surprised and proud of yourself when you realize that God has made recognizable changes in how you handle things. "The good person out of the good treasure of his heart produces good, and the evil person out of his evil treasure produces evil, for out of the abundance of the heart his mouth speaks" (Luke 6:45). Matthew 5:8 tells us, "Blessed are the pure in heart, for they shall see God." With the Holy Spirit indwelling you and living water pumping from the heart of God through your veins, the old man is gone and you are a new creature in Christ! (2 Corinthians 5:17).

So what can you do to avail yourself of the spiritual health improvements you experience after God's heart transplant? Exercise! You need spiritual exercise every day to keep your new heart strong. Stay in the Word of God, pray without ceasing, seek wise counsel, let go of old hurts, practice forgiveness, and ask the Holy Spirit to reveal to you anything in your character, nature, communications, or actions that is not pleasing to God.

If you do all those things faithfully, you will be a healthy Christian who can look in the mirror, smile, and thank God for His surgical expertise because you will know that

Your Heart Matters!

Your Heart Matters

1. What are the symptoms of a bad spiritual heart?

2. What limits do these symptoms and the root causes place on a person?

3. Give examples in your own spiritual development when "According to medicine, the heart transplant is immediate, but the mind transformation is progressive."

4. When did you know for sure that you were a new creature in Christ?

Soul Surgery Journal: My Heart's Notes

_____

_____

_____

_____

_____

_____

_____

_____

_____

_____

_____

_____

_____

_____

_____

CHAPTER 9

PILLOW TALK

I have stored up your Word in my heart,
that I might not sin against you.

Psalm 119:11, ESV

*I*t is always good thing to have scriptures of affirmation and comfort readily available when we need them. We may not recall the exact Bible address of a particular scripture, but if we know the meaning and hide it in our new hearts, we can call upon it in time of trouble. Here are some scriptures to help you in your Christian walk while embracing your new heart. Mediate on them in your quiet moments, and as you put your head on the pillow at night. Remember the goodness of God and the promises you have in His Word.

- Search me, Oh God, and know my heart; and see if there is any wicked way in me and lead in the way everlasting (Psalm 139:23-24).

- Teach me Your way, O Lord; I will walk in Your truth; Unite my heart to fear Your name. I will praise You, O Lord my God, with all my heart, and I will glorify Your name forevermore (Psalm 86:11-12).

- You should love the Lord your god with all your heart, with all your soul, and with all your strength (Deuteronomy 6:5).

- I will give you a new heart, and a new spirit I will put within you. And I will remove the heart of stone from your flesh and give you a heart of flesh (Ezekiel 36:26).

- Create in me a clean heart, O God and renew a steadfast spirit within me (Psalm 51:10).

- Let the words of my mouth and the meditations of my heart be acceptable in your sight (Psalm 19:14).

- And do not be conformed to this world, but be transformed by the renewing of your mind, that you may prove what is that right and good and perfect will of God (Romans 12:2).

- And to be renewed in the spirit of your minds, and to put on the new self, created after the likeness of God in true righteousness and holiness (Ephesians 4:23-24).

- Therefore, preparing your minds for action, and being sober-minded, set your hope fully on the grace that will be brought to you at the revelation of Jesus Christ (1 Peter 1:13).

I believe God commissioned me to spread the word that you can break free of the yoke of bondage you are under, whether from outside influences or self-inflicted. I cling to the Word and realize that I am a child of the Most High God, free of the enemy's grip when it comes to division, envy, jealousy, strive, and selfishness.

I am the anointed one in my family to stop the repeated trials and tribulations that have plagued my family for generations. The buck stops here because I can do all things through Christ who strengthens me. As a mother, I pray for my children and ask God to protect and shield them from the influences of my family's past, to open the eyes of their hearts and let the Holy Spirit lead them down righteous paths, and free them from the chains of poverty, fear, depression, cancer, low self-esteem, laziness, procrastination, lust, disrespect for the opposite sex, and other problems that have been handed down over generations.

You too can escape the repeated negative cycles and be free in Jesus Name. Your Heart Matters!

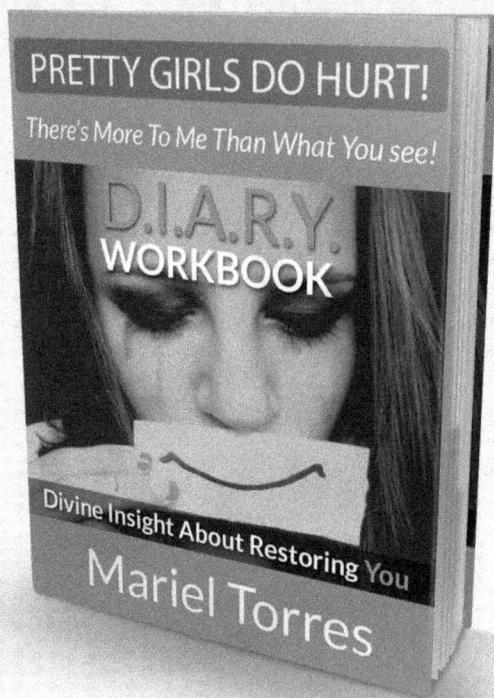

Note from the Publisher

Are you a first time author?

Not sure how to proceed to get your book published?
Want to keep all your rights and all your royalties?
Want it to look as good as a Top 10 publisher?
Need help with editing, layout, cover design?
Want it out there selling in 90 days or less?

Visit our website for some exciting new options!

www.chalfant-eckert-publishing.com